ULTIMA

FORD MUSTANG SHELBY GT350

By Tammy Gagne

Kaleidoscope

Minneapolis, MN

BIGFOOT BOOKS

The Quest for Discovery Never Ends

This edition is co-published by agreement between
Kaleidoscope and World Book, Inc.

Kaleidoscope Publishing, Inc.
6012 Blue Circle Drive
Minnetonka, MN 55343 U.S.A.

World Book, Inc.
180 North LaSalle St., Suite 900
Chicago IL 60601 U.S.A.

Kaleidoscope ISBNs
978-1-64519-029-5 (library bound)
978-1-64494-236-9 (paperback)
978-1-64519-129-2 (ebook)

World Book ISBN
978-0-7166-4330-2 (library bound)

Library of Congress Control Number
2019940227

Printed in the United States of America.

FIND ME
IF YOU CAN!

Bigfoot lurks within
one of the images in
this book. It's up to
you to find him!

TABLE OF
CONTENTS

CHAPTER 1

THAT'S A LOT OF HORSES!

Maggie had entered a contest. She didn't expect to win.
But it was fun to dream about. The winner got to drive
Maggie's favorite car. It was a 2019 Ford Mustang Shelby
GT350. They would drive it around a racetrack.

The 2019 Mustang Shelby GT350 is the latest in a long line of Mustang models.

She had gotten the good news in a letter. She won! She couldn't believe it. Now she sat behind the steering wheel. Maggie revved the engine. She was about to drive her dream car.

She thought about horses. A mustang is a kind of horse. But Maggie was thinking of horsepower. That's how engineers measure the power of a car's engine. They compare it to the power of running horses. Maggie had read articles about the Shelby GT350. They said the car had 526 horsepower. That was more than double the horsepower of Maggie's car.

The racetrack had no speed limit. Maggie could drive as fast as she wanted. She had read something exciting about the car. It could go from 0 to 60 miles per hour (97 km/h) in 4.3 seconds. She'd never driven a car that could **accelerate** that quickly. She wanted to test it for herself.

The Mustang Shelby GT350 comes in many colors.

FORD MUSTANG SHELBY GT350

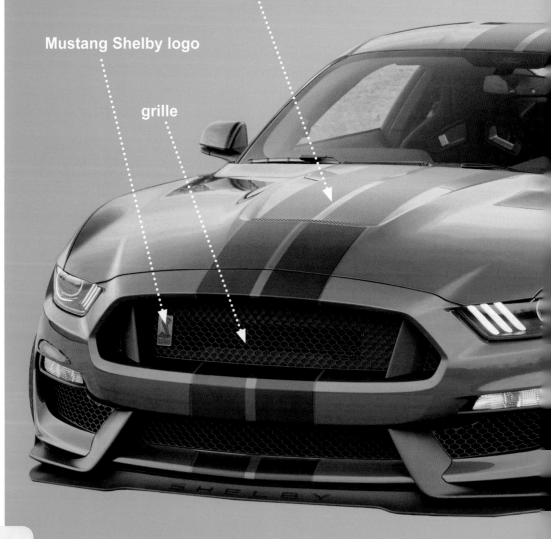

racing stripes

Mustang Shelby logo

grille

Maggie took her foot off the brake. She pressed the gas pedal. Maggie counted to herself. One, two, three . . . She glanced at the **speedometer**. The needle was climbing past 60. And it was still going. One moment she had been sitting still. The next she was zooming toward the track's first curve. The car handled as well as she had imagined. Maggie was at the finish line before she knew it. There was only one bad thing about the contest. The ride was over too soon!

rear spoiler

FUN FACT
The Shelby GT350 has a top speed of 200 miles per hour (322 km/h)!

high-performance tires

CHAPTER 2

Henry Ford changed the world of cars forever when he introduced the Model T.

FORD'S SPORTIEST SPORTS CAR

The year was 1908. Henry Ford introduced the Model T. It made Ford Motor Company famous. Ford added many more models over the years. But few have been as **iconic** as the Mustang Shelby. This model was named after Carroll Shelby.

Shelby was a flight instructor during World War II (1939–1945). Then the war ended. He became interested in cars. He became a race car driver. He loved zooming around a track. Shelby got sick. He had to stop racing. But he didn't stop loving cars. He wanted to build race cars.

The name may have stayed the same, but the Shelby GT350 has changed a lot since 1965.

Shelby was always thinking. He kept a notepad by his bed. Sometimes he woke up with a good idea. He wrote it down. Then he would remember it in the morning. One night he had a dream. It was about a snake called a cobra. He decided to make a car called the Cobra.

The Ford Motor Company saw the Cobra. Ford knew Shelby could improve the Ford Mustang. Shelby took the job. The result was the first "Shelby Mustang" in 1965. Shelby designed many more models for Ford. The cobra became the Mustang Shelby's **emblem**.

The cobra fit the Mustang Shelby. It was a powerful car. It had 306 horsepower. This was more than the Ford Mustang. The Mustang Shelby would be Ford's sportiest car.

MUSTANG OR MUSTANG SHELBY?

A Mustang and a Mustang Shelby may appear similar. But a closer look can help tell them apart. The Shelby version has the famous cobra emblem. The Shelby also has two racing stripes. They go down the middle of the car.

Carroll Shelby

Shelby made improvements to the standard Mustang. The Shelby model had better steering. It also had wider wheels and high-speed Goodyear tires. The Shelby was made for the road. But it handled like a race car.

The Mustang Shelby changed over the years. Each new version included improvements. The Shelby GT350 isn't just the sportiest Ford on the road. It is one of the sportiest cars from any automaker.

FUN FACT

Ford made its 10 millionth Mustang in 2018.

FLAT ROCK WELCOMES THE SHELBY GT350 & GT350R

The Mustang Shelby is manufactured in Las Vegas. The cars are then assembled more than 2,000 miles (3,200 km) away in Flat Rock, Michigan.

Where the Shelby GT350 Is Made

1 **Las Vegas, Nevada:** Shelby American headquarters, where Mustang Shelby parts are manufactured

2 **Dearborn, Michigan:** Ford headquarters

3 **Flat Rock, Michigan:** Flat Rock Plant, where Mustang Shelbys are assembled

CHAPTER 3

THE SHELBY GT350'S DEFINING FEATURES

Juan's mouth dropped open. His parents had bought a Mustang Shelby GT350. They promised to pick him up from school in it. He knew it would be pretty. But he didn't expect it to look like a race car! He wondered if it drove like one.

His father told him it was a supercar. This meant that it accelerated quickly. It performed well on the road. It also meant that it could drive fast.

"Put your seatbelt on," Juan's mother said. "We're going for a ride."

The Shelby GT350 appeared at the 2014 Los Angeles Auto Show.

The car had only two doors. Juan's dad got out of the car. He pushed his seat forward. Juan crawled into the tiny backseat. He picked up a brochure on the seat. It said that the Shelby GT350 had a **V8** engine. His mother turned onto the road. He could feel the engine's power. She took the on-ramp to the highway. Now he could hear the power, too.

Features like stability control make the Shelby GT350 safer.

The road curved. The tires hugged the road as his mother steered. Last summer, the family's car skidded during a rainstorm. His dad said that wouldn't happen in the Shelby. It had **stability** control. This helped prevent skidding.

THE SHELBY GT350
IN DETAIL

Height: 4.5 feet (1.4 m)

Width: 6.8 feet (2.1 m)

Length: 15.8 feet (4.8 m)

COST: $59,140

Weight: 3,805 pounds (1,726 kg)

Top Speed: 200 miles per hour (322 km/h)

Time from 0–60 miles per hour (0–97 km/h): 4.3 seconds

Juan saw a touch screen up front. He wished he was big enough to sit up there. His mom turned on the radio. His favorite song played from the car's twelve speakers. The sound system sounded better than his headphones.

"Do you want to try the heated seat?" his father asked his mother.

"Yes, please!" She sounded so excited. Now Juan really looked forward to sitting in that front seat.

FUN FACT

All GT350s come with touch screen controls.

MAGNERIDE

Regular cars are comfortable. But they don't handle like a sports car. The 2019 Shelby GT350 offers both. It has an option called MagneRide. This feature keeps the wheels in contact with the road. It makes the ride feel smoother.

CHAPTER 4

THE MUSTANG SHELBY'S FUTURE

"Is that the story about the 2019 Mustang Shelby GT350?" Rayan asked his sister Anika.

"It is," she answered. She kept her eyes on her magazine. "It sounds amazing."

Their uncle Raj had taught them about the Mustang Shelby. He had an older GT350. Raj hoped to buy a brand-new GT350 one day. But he wasn't going to sell his first model. He loved it too much.

He also thought it might be worth a lot of money. Many Mustang Shelby fans collected older models.

The Shelby GT350 has special tires that help it stay on the track.

Shelby GT350 owners can attend Track Attack, a high-performance driving experience, to get the most out of driving the GT350.

"Raj told me the new model is beautiful," Rayan said.

Anika agreed. "Ford asked a race car driver for help. He told them how make it better. There's a new **spoiler**. The Shelby GT350 also has special tires."

"What about under the hood?" Rayan asked. "That's what really matters."

"The engine is exclusive. It's a V8," his sister replied. "And the **cabin** has lots of technology. They want the car to weigh as little as possible."

"Of course," Rayan said. "Weighing less helps it move faster." He acted like he knew more about cars than anyone. But Anika also knew her fair share.

The 2019 Shelby GT350's spoiler makes it more aerodynamic.

"I know," she said. "The car's **aerodynamic** design helps with that."

Rayan rolled his eyes. Anika was better at remembering the big words.

"The Mustang Shelby has been around a long time," Anika said. "I wonder what it will look like when we're adults."

"I don't know," Rayan said. "I would just like to see this one. Are you done with that magazine yet?"

"In a minute," Anika teased. "I want to dream about owning a Shelby a bit longer."

WHAT MAKES THE GT350'S DESIGN AERODYNAMIC?

Air resistance can slow down a supercar. The designers know this. That's why they pay close attention to the car's shape and size. Shelby GT350 designers are careful. They can't make it too wide or large. Air moves around the 2019 Shelby GT350 easily. The car's rear spoiler also helps reduce air resistance.

FUN FACT

The 2019 Shelby GT350 is also available in a race version called the GT350R.

BEYOND
THE BOOK

**After reading the book, it's time to think about what you learned.
Try the following exercises to jumpstart your ideas.**

THINK

DIFFERENT SOURCES. Think about what types of sources you could find on the Mustang Shelby GT350. What could you find in a magazine? What could you learn at a dealership? How could each of the sources be useful in its own way?

CREATE

PRIMARY SOURCES. A primary source is an original document, photograph, or interview. Make a list of different primary sources you might be able to find about the Mustang Shelby GT350. What new information might you learn from these sources?

SHARE

WHAT'S YOUR OPINION? Juan's dad says that the Mustang Shelby GT350 is considered a supercar. Do you agree or disagree with this position? Use evidence from the text to support your answer. Share your position and evidence with a friend. Does your friend agree with you?

GROW

REAL-LIFE RESEARCH. What places could you visit to learn more about the Mustang Shelby GT350? What other things could you learn while you were there?

RESEARCH NINJA

Visit *www.ninjaresearcher.com/0295* to learn how
to take your research skills and book report writing to the next level!

RESEARCH

DIGITAL LITERACY TOOLS

SEARCH LIKE A PRO
Learn about how to use search engines to find useful websites.

FACT OR FAKE?
Discover how you can tell a trusted website from an untrustworthy resource.

TEXT DETECTIVE
Explore how to zero in on the information you need most.

SHOW YOUR WORK
Research responsibly— learn how to cite sources.

WRITE

GET TO THE POINT
Learn how to express your main ideas.

PLAN OF ATTACK
Learn prewriting exercises and create an outline.

DOWNLOADABLE REPORT FORMS

FURTHER RESOURCES

BOOKS

Lanier, Wendy Hinote. *Sports Cars*. Focus Readers, 2017.

Mason, Paul. *American Supercars: Dodge, Chevrolet, Ford*. PowerKids Press, 2019.

Oachs, Emily Rose. *Ford Mustang Shelby GT350*. Bellwether Media, 2017.

WEBSITES

Factsurfer.com gives you a safe, fun way to find more information.

1. Go to www.factsurfer.com.

2. Enter "Ford Mustang Shelby GT350" into the search box and click 🔍.

3. Select your book cover to see a list of related websites.

GLOSSARY

accelerate: To accelerate means to go faster. The Mustang Shelby GT350 can accelerate from 0 to 60 miles per hour (97 km/h) in 4.3 seconds.

aerodynamic: An aerodynamic design reduces the drag, or pull, on a car as it moves through air. The GT350's rear spoiler is part of its aerodynamic design.

cabin: The cabin is the inside of a car, where the driver and passengers sit. The cabin of the 2019 Mustang Shelby GT350 can seat four people.

emblem: An emblem is a symbolic object that often appears alongside a car's name on the vehicle. The Mustang Shelby's emblem is a cobra.

iconic: Something that is iconic is greatly admired or respected. The Mustang Shelby is an iconic sports car.

speedometer: A speedometer is a display on the dashboard that tells how fast a vehicle is going. The driver saw on the speedometer that he was going too fast.

spoiler: A spoiler is a fin or wing that changes the airflow around the car. The 2019 Shelby GT350 has a spoiler to make it more aerodynamic.

stability: Stability is the ability to stay firmly on the ground. The Mustang Shelby's stability control prevented an accident in the storm.

V8: A V8 engine has 8 cylinders in the shape of a *V*. The Ford Mustang Shelby GT350 has a V8 engine.

INDEX

PHOTO CREDITS

ABOUT THE AUTHOR

Tammy Gagne has written dozens of books for both adults and children. Her recent titles include *Quarterbacks* from the NFL's Greatest Players series and *Dodge Viper SRT* from the Ultimate Supercars series. She lives in northern New England with her husband, son, and a menagerie of pets.